5K Fury: 10 Proven Steps to Get You to the Finish Line in 9 Weeks or Less!

by Scott O. Morton

All rights reserved. This book or parts thereof may not be reproduced in any form, stored in any retrieval system, or transmitted in any form by any means—electronic, mechanical, photocopy, recording, or otherwise—without prior written consent of the publisher, except as provided by United States of America copyright law. For reproduction rights, write to the publisher, at "Attention: Reproduction Rights," at the address below.

© 2017 by LERK Publishing, LLC. All rights reserved.

LERK Publishing, LLC

Cover design: LERK Publishing, LLC

ISBN: **978-1-947010-05-5**

Follow me on Facebook and Twitter:

Twitter: @BeginR2FinishR

Facebook: facebook.com/BeginnerToFinisher/

Website: www.halfmarathonforbeginners.com

Email: scottmorton@halfmarathonforbeginners.com

To my father, Richard
(Coach, Entrepreneur, Visionary)

Medical Disclaimer

The information in this book is meant to supplement, not replace, proper half marathon training. A sport involving speed, equipment, balance and environmental factors, and running, will involve some inherent risk. The authors and publisher advise readers to take full responsibility for their safety and know their limits. Before practicing the skills described in this book, be sure that your equipment is well maintained, and do not take risks beyond your level of experience, aptitude, training, and comfort level.

Other books by Scott O. Morton

Beginner to Finisher Series:

Available Now:

Book 1: *Why New Runners Fail: 26 Ultimate Tips You Should Know Before You Start Running!*

Book 2: *5K Fury: 10 Proven Steps to Get You to the Finish Line in 9 weeks or less!*

Book 3: *10K Titan: Push Beyond the 5K in 6 Weeks or Less!*

Book 4: *Beginner's Guide to Half Marathons: A Simple Step-By-Step Solution to Get You to the Finish Line in 12 Weeks!*

Coming Soon:

Book 5: *Marathon Motivator: A Simple Step-By-Step Solution to get you to the Finish line in 20 Weeks!*

Why I Wrote This Book

I wrote this book for anyone with a burning desire to take up running as an occasional hobby or launch themselves all the way to marathon training! I truly want everyone that reads this book to complete at least one 5K. If I can help at least one person achieve this goal, then all the time put into this book will be worthwhile.

This book is designed for anyone with a desire to complete a 5K. If you follow the steps outlined in this book, you will achieve this goal. This book is not intended to be a guide for the experienced runner. Increasing your speed and decreasing your finish times are not covered in this book. Tons of other books and websites cover beating your personal best records and reducing your overall 5k, 10k, half marathon, and marathon run times.

Injuries & Medical Conditions

If you have sports related injuries, I highly suggest that you talk to a medical professional to determine if you are fit enough to endure running. Not seeking medical advice could further exacerbate an existing injury. I am not a legal or medical professional, nor am I offering any legal or medical advice. One last time, if you're injured or have medical conditions that prevent you from taking on a rigorous running training program, please seek the opinion of a licensed physician before participating in any physical training. While the training required for a half marathon is not nearly as difficult as the training for a full marathon, it will still push both your mental and physical capabilities.

What's in This Book

5K Fury will cover the bare bones basics of what is required to complete a 5K. This book will not cover any advanced running techniques. Its target audience is for beginner runners who want to take on the challenge of their first 5K.

Assumptions

Before you dive into this book, I'm assuming the following:

- You have a desire to walk or run your first 5K.
- You will stick to a training schedule that is provided in this book or elsewhere.
- You can walk at least two consecutive miles without becoming winded. How fast you walk them doesn't matter.

If you are having trouble walking one mile without becoming winded, I recommend working your way up to 1 mile before following the training in this book. You can go ahead and read this book first, but I would follow the schedule below until you can walk at least one mile without being winded or sore.

Week #	Training
1	Walk 3 days a week for a minimum of 10 minutes or 0.5 miles.
2	Walk 3 days a week for a minimum of 20 minutes or 1 mile.
3	Walk 3 days a week for a minimum of 30 minutes or 1.5 miles.
4	Walk 3 days a week for a minimum of 40 minutes or 2.0 miles.

The training mentioned above can be adjusted to suit your needs. If you can already walk a mile, then adjust accordingly. The most important part of pre-training is to condition your body to walk or run the distance of a 5K. With that in mind, take it nice and slow. Once you can walk at least 2 miles in one training session, you can proceed to the main training plan located in the last section of this book.

Step 1: Select a Race Date

#1 Reason Why Runners Don't Finish a 5K

If I had to choose the number one reason why runners don't complete a 5K I would have to go with not selecting a race date. Without a race date, you haven't created a running goal to shoot for beyond the goal of trying to run 3.1 miles. After you select your race date, the number two reason for not completing a 5K would be not signing up for the race date you selected.

Set the Training Start Date

After you select your race date, tell the world about your goal to finish a 5K. Tell your running partner, if you have one, and most importantly tell yourself. Write the goal down. Send yourself an email. Schedule a text message to yourself congratulating you on starting the training program. Once you have determined your race date, you need to work backward to determine when your start date for your 5K training should begin.

For example, if your race were on Saturday, November 25th, 2017, then you would count backward 9 weeks which would place your start week on, Monday, September 25th, 2017.

Selecting Your Race

Choosing a favorable season as well as selecting a flat course will increase your overall race experience. In Texas, the spring and fall are great times to run. California is an ideal location to train and race due to the year-round fair weather. Many other states are good places to run as well. For a first-time runner, I want you to have a positive race experience. I don't recommend your first 5K to be in an environment that the temperature is greater than 80 degrees. Excessive heat will slow you down and increase your overall finish time.

For a list of 5K races, please visit the website Running In The USA.

Action Steps

- Select your race date.
- Sign-up for your race.

Step 2: Prepare Thyself for Running

Runner's Mindset

Getting past the fear of running is one of the biggest hurdles of completing any running race. I'm going to let you in on a big secret that helped me get past my fear of having to run. The secret is you don't have to run the entire race. Wow, what a secret. It's true. There will be many participants in a 5K that will run the entire race and not stop for water. If this is your goal, great! If you just want to cross the finish line regardless of walking or running or a combination of both, that works too! Once I realized that you don't have to run the entire distance, the fear of running vanished, instantly. My mind had found a chink in the armor. I'm by no means a super athlete, just an average person with high beliefs that I could run. I hope that this encourages you to finish your first 5K no matter what your age is. If I can do it, so can you.

For a small pool of runners, finishing a 5K or a 10K can be accomplished with little or no training at all. The amount of training needed depends greatly on your age, health, and fitness level. For most new runners, following a training plan will get you to your goal faster and injury free better than simply winging it. Shield yourself from remarks such as, "you really can't say you finished a 5K if you don't run it." Nonsense! Put on your bulletproof, remark ricocheting armor and forge onward. The one thing I ask of you starting today is to start telling yourself that you are training for a 5K. You are no longer running for the sake of exercise. You are running to train your body to complete your first 5K.

Many things that I go over in this book are solely my opinion. Every training schedule discussed within this book has been used by me at one point in my running career beginning with 5Ks through a marathon. There are several different schools of thought when it comes to how much running per week it takes to train for each race. There are different nutrition guides, shoe strategies, running miles per week, etc. When it comes to training schedules, there isn't a one size fits all schedule. Some things work better for other people, and some things will work better for you. There is, however, one common thing agreed upon by almost all runners - you have to believe in yourself and believe that you are a runner. Without this firmly ingrained in your head, you are exposing yourself to your minds ability to defeat your willpower. By telling yourself that you're a runner, it's almost as if you are permitting your mind to tell your body that you are a runner which in turn releases built up tension surrounding the idea of running. I'm not telling you this to discourage you. I'm telling you this to prepare you for the mental battle of running. Will there be days that your mind will sneak up on you and attack your running motivation? Of course, there will be. Telling yourself that you're a runner, however, will help minimize these mind sneak attacks. One week at a time, one day at a time, one mile at a time, and one step at a time will get you to the finish line.

The Power of Affirmations

When I first trained for my 5k and 10k races I had no prior knowledge of affirmations. Affirmations are positive action phrases you repeat to yourself on a daily basis to brainwash your mind. I made a list of affirmations that I repeated daily while training for races. Every time before I ran I would tell myself these affirmations:

- I'm a runner.
- I'm training for a 5K.
- I'm going to complete my 5K training.
- I'm going to cross the finish line.

After I finished a long run, I would take the affirmations one step further and visualize myself crossing the 5K finish line.

I contributed most of my success to believing in myself and knowing that failure wasn't an option. By repeating daily affirmations, you can trick your mind into accomplishing almost anything. Affirmations might seem a bit childish. However, they work if you are true to yourself and your level of commitment. Affirmations can be anything that you want them to be, old childhood dreams, new experiences, etc. The power is in the affirmation and hearing yourself say them. Give them a try for a week and see what happens.

Take a moment and write down a list of at least five affirmations. Title the list "Running Affirmations." Refer to this list every day, especially right before you go on a run.

Motivation

Why do some people finish marathons and other don't? I believe it comes down to self-motivation and determination. Self-motivation, while probably the strongest of any other form of motivation, is not the only source of motivation. There are several different types of motivation. Three types of motivation that I believe are the most influential come from social media, running partners and yourself.

Social Media

Social media can help keep you focused and motivated by your circle of friends. You can post running times and screenshots of your runs to social media to let your circle of friends comment and cheer you on. Social media will help perk you up when you have a day that you just don't feel like running.

Running Partners

Running partners are the next best thing to yourself keeping you motivated. They train with you. They give you feedback. They help you stay on pace. They push you when you have no more energy. Partners also help you stay accountable for following through with your goal.

One caveat to a running partner is that if they lack self-motivation, they aren't going to be of much help motivating you.

<u>Yourself</u>

Self-motivation is by far the most powerful source of motivation. You know yourself better than anyone else. You are custom to knowing how your mind and body function. If you don't feel like running one day, tell yourself that you will just run a half a mile. After you run a half mile, tell yourself that you will just run one mile. By pushing yourself just a little bit, you can trick your mind into running.

Your motivation could be to get healthy and fit. Also, you could be motivated just to prove to yourself that you can finish a 5K or to donate to a worthy cause. Whatever the motivation is, you and only you will finish the race.

Action Steps

- Create your affirmations.
- Repeat your affirmations daily and before each run.

5K Fury

Step 3: Gather Needed Running Gear

Shoes

Don't skimp out on your shoes. Could you complete a 5K in Crocs? Sure. Do I recommend it? No, especially if you are planning on running it. I would invest some money in at least one good pair of running socks and running shoes. Some of the best brands of shoes for running include:

Adidas
Asics
Brooks
Nike
Mizuno
Saucony

Pronation

Depending on what your pronation is, you will need either a shoe that is built for flexibility, stabilization, or comfort. To determine which pronation you exhibit, you can use the wet feet on concrete test. Simply dip your feet in water and run a few quick strides across the concrete. Take a picture or just study your foot mark.

Entire foot showing - over - motion-control (flat feet)
Normal foot showing - normal - stability shoes (average)
Arch barely visible - under - cushioned shoes (high arch)

Pronation becomes more important when you start to routinely run much longer distances such as 6 miles and beyond. For a beginner runner, you can probably get by with some average cushioned shoes unless you already know that you are flat-footed. If you're flat footed, then you need to purchase motion-control shoes.

Clothing

Your shorts and shirt should be relatively loose fitting. If it's hot, you might prefer to wear a tank top to keep you cool on your runs. If it's cold outside you should dress for the weather accordingly. However, even when it's cold outside, after your body has warmed up, you will want to start shedding clothes. If you are hot natured, which I am, the best thing to do on cold running days is to run in a circuit or loopback. If you run in a circuit, you can ditch your clothes after warming up and come back by on the same route and pick them up.

Socks

Find a good pair of socks that won't cause blisters. Balega socks are notoriously known for preventing blisters. They are a little expensive, but in my opinion, they are worth every penny. Balega socks are ultra-light by design, and you don't even notice that the sock is on your foot most of the time.

Some runners will prefer compression socks. Studies have shown that runners that wear compression socks tend to have less cramping and better endurance. The only caveat is that compression socks only help marginally until you get into the long-distance running of 5 miles plus. Compression socks cover most of the calf and normally sit right underneath the kneecap. Either type of sock will do, but in my opinion, for a 5K, neither is better than the other, so it comes down to personal preference.

Wearables

Running with your smartphone is an ideal choice for many runners. On a smartphone, you can listen to music and track your run time and pace. There are hundreds of running apps you can install on your phone to do this. Couch 2 5K is probably one of the more popular running apps for 5Ks. If you do choose to run with a smartphone, I would buy an armband case that can be strapped to your forearm or upper arm. If you want to hold your phone in your hands, I would alternate hands during your runs every mile or every 5 minutes. If you continuously use the same hand to hold your phone while you run, you are opening yourself up to improper balance injuries because of the added weight during your gait cycle. Your gait cycle is the locomotion that your legs and body make to complete one leg stride from lift off to touch down.

Apple 2 sports watches, Garmin VivoActive watches, and Fitbits are alternatives to bringing your phone along for a run. One drawback is that you don't have a phone in case of an emergency and the other is that you don't have music to listen to. One fix is to buy a small MP3 player such as a Clip-on Sandisk Sports MP3 Player and load it up with MP3s. I currently run with Garmin VivoActive HR and a Sandisk MP3 player. I don't like the extra bulk and weight of a smartphone. Again this comes down to preference and what kind of wearables you want to dawn.

Other

When I run, I have to wear sunglasses. Sunglasses do the obvious by helping reduce the sun in your eyes. However, I find they serve a second equal purpose. Sunglasses help block the wind in your eyes. On a windy day, you will beg for sunglasses to help prevent your eyes from tearing up when you run.

I sweat a lot when I run, so I have to wear a headband. Females that have long hair will probably want to tie back their hair when they run.

Most importantly, if it's sunny, don't forget your sunblock.

Action Steps

- Buy some socks and shoes.
- Buy some running clothes if you don't have any.
- Use an app or wearable to track your run time and pace.

5K Fury

Step 4: Proper Running Posture

Tension is Thy Runner's Enemy

Body tension is your enemy. When your body is tense, you are spending extra energy because your body is having to hold your muscles in that flexed position. Try relaxing your shoulders and concentrate on breathing for a couple of cycles. By breathing normally, you will help ease tension in the body within seconds.

Foot Strikes

Your feet need to move in short quick steps and land underneath your hips. Your feet shouldn't land out in front of your hips.

Many different studies have tried to give scientific evidence over where you should land on your foot while running. There are three different locations on the feet where foot to ground impact occurs. The Forefoot, Mid-foot, and Heel. If you ever take the time to research the topic on foot striking, you will see just how conflicting reports are on the subject. In my opinion, I believe there is no difference on where your foot should land. The ideal location for your foot to land is the mid-foot. Heel strikers have a slightly higher tendency to over-stride, which is not good. As a new runner, I wouldn't get too hung up on this topic, especially if you are only running a 5K for now. If you start to become extremely sore or running becomes extremely painful in areas of your feet, you will want to get your running gait cycle analyzed by a running store.

Arms

Most runners don't think of their hand placement during a run. Your arms should sway back and forth naturally without tightening up your fists and pulling them in close to the body. The arms should never reach beyond 90 degrees on the upswing in front of your body. For best practice, your arms shouldn't rise above your belly button on the upswing.

Head

Try to keep your head lifted up. You will be able to run further, allowing your breathing to come and go with ease. If your head is squished into your chest, like you see some runners do, you're not releasing as much carbon dioxide as you should be, causing your breathing to become more difficult. When your head is lifted and looking straight forward, your airways for breathing are in an optimal position.

Chest

Your body should be slightly leaned forward with any momentum leaning into the forward traveling motion. Your breath should be a deep breath in and a deep breath out all the while running anywhere from 10 - 14 steps.

Back

Keep your back straight and upright. Relax your shoulders. Don't straighten your back to the extent that it is a plank, which feeds tension.

No-Nos

If you notice you have a bounce in your step, you need to have someone record you so that you can watch yourself running. The more bounce in your step, the more impact you will create for the landing foot after takeoff. It's a good idea to watch elite runners in the front of the pack run a race. You will notice that most of their running almost looks like they're gliding. Their feet are extremely close to the ground, and their bodies don't bounce up and down with each stride. If you tend to bounce when you're running, then your body is running at a disadvantage. Your body and energy will wear out faster than someone that runs with minimal vertical oscillation (bounce in your step).

Action Steps

- Head up.
- Chest out, with your body leaning slightly forward.
- Back straight.
- Arms should swing naturally, not above the belly button.
- Relax your shoulders.
- Your feet should land over your hip not out in front.
- Don't over-stride.
- Don't bounce while running.

5K Fury

Step 5: Warming Up & Cooling Down

Warming Up

Warming up for a 5k should take less than 5 minutes. You do not want to perform static stretching before running unless you are stiff or sore. If you are sore, this may be caused by not properly stretching after your last run. Remember to use a foam roller as part of your cooldown routine to help alleviate soreness and stiffness.

Dynamic stretches can include:
- Leg swings
- Walking knee raises
- Walking lunges
- Light jogging

Cooling Down

Proper cooling down and stretching is equally important as warming up. I use the following cool down guidelines. These are minimum distances that I walk after my runs. Most of the time I will walk two miles after each run so that I can unwind my legs and stretch.

Distance Ran	Cooldown (miles)
1-3	0.5
4-6	1
7-9	1.25
10-12	1.5

When performing static stretching you want to hold and release. Do not bounce while holding the stretch. Hold the stretch anywhere from 20 seconds to 2 minutes. Stretch and use your foam roller to help with soreness.

Static stretches can include:
- Standing quad
- Standing calf raises
- Hip revolutions
- Wall calf
- Bent hamstring

Rest

Adequate rest is needed just as much as your actual running hours and miles for training. After your runs, your body needs time to rebuild and repair the damage taken during your runs. It takes your legs up to 24 hours after each run over 2 miles to repair. Your body continues to build your muscles during the rest of the week's runs. Depending on your age, you should be getting an adequate amount of sleep each night. On average the human adult needs anywhere from 7 to 8 hours of sleep. During your training, you need to shoot for getting at least 7 hours of sleep a night.

Action Steps

- Before you run only perform dynamic stretching unless you are still sore after performing the stretches.
- Post-run you will want to perform several hold and release static stretches to help your body recover.
- Get adequate rest during your training cycle.

5K Fury

Step 6: Eat Like a Runner

Pre-Run

Before your runs, you will need to get into the habit of trying to eat at least two hours before your run. If you eat a burrito and then immediately attempt to run for thirty minutes, your body might disagree with your decision.

Your pre-run fuel should involve some carbohydrate such as a couple of pieces of bread or an energy bar. Sip on water but avoid the temptation to guzzle 12 ounces right before you run.

Post-Run

After your runs replenish your body with something light like a banana, an apple, or a light protein shake. Drink water and avoid drinking Gatorade altogether. Gatorade serves a purpose, but it's not vital for short distance races unless you lose a lot of fluid through sweating. A sodium and electrolyte replacement is needed when you run longer races such as half marathons because your body sweats out more sodium.

Losing Weight

If one of the other primary reasons for running a 5K

is to lose weight, then you need to pay close attention to

the following. Nothing has changed in the scientific community about losing weight and gaining weight. Your body, on a daily basis, needs between 2000 and 2500 calories a day to maintain your current weight. Having said that you would be surprised at how many new runners will run 1 or 2 miles and then consume a double cheeseburger and a side of fries. Weight loss doesn't work this way. Let's break down two examples:

To lose one pound of weight you have to burn 3,500 calories. The only way to increase the rate at which you burn calories, without artificial supplements, is to either consume fewer calories or burn more calories. Thankfully, there are tons of apps on the market that will help you achieve this. Living Strong, My Fitness Pal, Lose it!, and many others.

Example #1 - Gaining Weight

Sally's recommended daily caloric intake is around 2000 calories. All of her meals for the day equal 2,600 calories. She manages to run 3 miles for the day, which burns about 150 calories a mile. Her total caloric surplus would be 150 calories.

+ 2,600 calories consumed
- 2,000 calorie budget
-    450 calories burnt running

---

150 calories surplus (a marginal weight **gain**)

If she continues this daily eating pattern each day for two weeks, she will have **gained roughly 1/2 a pound.**
(150 calories * 14 days = 2,100 calories. To lose 1 pound of body weight you have to burn 3,500 calories.)

Example #2 - Losing Weight

Susan's recommended daily caloric intake is around 2300 calories. All of her meals for the day equal 2,450 calories. She manages to run 3 miles for the day, which burns about 150 calories a mile. Her total caloric deficit would be 250 calories.

+ 2,450 calories consumed
- 2,300 calorie budget
-    450 calories burnt running

---

250 calories deficit (a marginal weight **loss**)

If she continues this daily eating pattern each day for two weeks, she will have **lost roughly 1 pound.**
(250 calorie deficit * 14 days = 3,500 calories. To lose 1 pound of body weight you have to burn 3,500 calories.)

Action Steps

- Pre-run - eat light carbs such as bread or a protein bar.
- Post-run - eat some fruit or a protein shake.
- To lose weight, you must either consume fewer calories or burn more calories.

Step 7: Training Schedule

Training - Week 1

Monday	**Rest.** Take it easy. Don't run. If you need to exercise, I recommend a walk for no longer than 30 minutes.
Tuesday	**Walk 4 minutes and run 1 minute. Repeat 6 times.**
Wednesday	**Walk 4 minutes and run 1 minute. Repeat 6 times.**
Thursday	**Walk 4 minutes and run 1 minute. Repeat 6 times.**
Friday	**Rest.** Fridays are important rest days. For your muscles to grow stronger, they need rest. Feel free to walk for a few miles. Try not to drink alcohol the night before your Saturday runs. The first four weeks are fairly easy. Week five and beyond become increasingly difficult.
Saturday	**Walk 3 minutes and run 2 minutes. Repeat 6 times.**
Sunday	**Rest.** For beginner runners, this day needs to be kept at a mild rest day. If your body feels good, then go ahead and do some form of cross-training for 30 to 60 minutes.

Tuesday, Wednesday, Thursday, Saturday: If you can easily hold a conversation with someone, then you are running at the right pace. When you walk, try to maintain a pace no slower than 15 minutes/a mile (4 mph).

Training - Week 2

Monday	**Rest.** Take it easy. Don't run. If you need to exercise, I recommend a walk for no longer than 30 minutes.
Tuesday	**Walk 3 minutes and run 2 minutes. Repeat 6 times.**
Wednesday	**Walk 3 minutes and run 2 minutes. Repeat 6 times.**
Thursday	**Walk 3 minutes and run 2 minutes. Repeat 6 times.**
Friday	**Rest.** Fridays are important rest days. For your muscles to grow stronger, they need rest. Feel free to walk for a few miles. Try not to drink alcohol the night before your Saturday runs. The first four weeks are fairly easy. Week five and beyond become increasingly difficult.
Saturday	**Walk 3 minutes and run 2 minutes. Repeat 6 times.**
Sunday	**Rest.** For beginner runners, this day needs to be kept at a mild rest day. If your body feels good, then go ahead and do some form of cross-training for 30 to 60 minutes.

Tuesday, Wednesday, Thursday, Saturday: If you can easily hold a conversation with someone, then you are running at the right pace. When you walk, try to maintain a pace no slower than 15 minutes/a mile (4 mph).

Training - Week 3

Monday	**Rest.** Take it easy. Don't run. If you need to exercise, I recommend a walk for no longer than 30 minutes.
Tuesday	**Walk 3 minutes and run 2 minutes. Repeat 6 times.**
Wednesday	**Walk 2 minutes and run 4 minutes. Repeat 3 times.**
Thursday	**Walk 3 minutes and run 2 minutes. Repeat 6 times.**
Friday	**Rest.** Fridays are important rest days. For your muscles to grow stronger, they need rest. Feel free to walk for a few miles. Try not to drink alcohol the night before your Saturday runs. The first four weeks are fairly easy. Week five and beyond become increasingly difficult.
Saturday	**Walk 3 minutes and run 6 minutes. Repeat 3 times.**
Sunday	**Rest.** For beginner runners, this day needs to be kept at a mild rest day. If your body feels good, then go ahead and do some form of cross training for 30 to 60 minutes.

Tuesday, Wednesday, Thursday, Saturday: If you can easily hold a conversation with someone, then you are running at the right pace. When you walk, try to maintain a pace no slower than 15 minutes/a mile (4 mph).

Training - Week 4

Monday	**Rest.** Take it easy. Don't run. If you need to exercise, I recommend a walk for no longer than 30 minutes.
Tuesday	**Walk 2 minutes and run 3 minutes. Repeat 6 times.**
Wednesday	**Walk 2 minutes and run 6 minutes. Repeat 4 times.**
Thursday	**Walk 2 minutes and run 3 minutes. Repeat 6 times.**
Friday	**Rest.** Fridays are important rest days. For your muscles to grow stronger, they need rest. Feel free to walk for a few miles. Try not to drink alcohol the night before your Saturday runs. The first four weeks are easy. Week five and beyond become increasingly difficult.
Saturday	**Walk 3 minutes and run 8 minutes. Repeat 2 times.**
Sunday	**Rest.** For beginner runners, this day needs to be kept at a mild rest day. If your body feels good, then go ahead and do some form of cross-training for 30 to 60 minutes.

Tuesday, Wednesday, Thursday, Saturday: If you can easily hold a conversation with someone, then you are running at the right pace. When you walk, try to maintain a pace no slower than 15 minutes/a mile (4 mph).

Training - Week 5

Monday	**Rest.** Take it easy. Don't run. If you need to exercise, I recommend a walk for no longer than 30 minutes.
Tuesday	**Walk 2 minutes and run 3 minutes. Repeat 6 times.**
Wednesday	**Walk 1 minute and run 8 minutes. Repeat 3 times.**
Thursday	**Walk 2 minutes and run 3 minutes. Repeat 6 times.**
Friday	**Rest.** Fridays are important rest days. For your muscles to grow stronger, they need rest. Feel free to walk for a few miles. Try not to drink alcohol the night before your Saturday runs. The first four weeks are fairly easy. Week five and beyond become increasingly difficult.
Saturday	**Run 12 minutes.**
Sunday	**Rest.** For beginner runners, this day needs to be kept at a mild rest day. If your body feels good, then go ahead and do some form of cross-training for 30 to 60 minutes.

Tuesday, Wednesday, Thursday: If you can easily hold a conversation with someone, then you are running at the right pace. When you walk, try to maintain a pace no slower than 15 minutes/a mile (4 mph).

Saturdays: Weeks 5-9 will start pushing your limits. Get plenty of sleep the night before. Starting this week, it's important to remember to stretch after your run sessions. If you get tired during a longer duration run, walk for 1/10 mile or 2-3 minutes then speed back up.

Training - Week 6

Monday	**Rest.** Take it easy. Don't run. If you need to exercise, I recommend a walk for no longer than 30 minutes.
Tuesday	**Walk 1 minute and run 4 minutes. Repeat 6 times.**
Wednesday	**Walk 1 minute and run 10 minutes. Repeat 3 times.**
Thursday	**Walk 1 minute and run 4 minutes. Repeat 6 times.**
Friday	**Rest.** Fridays are important rest days. For your muscles to grow stronger, they need rest. Feel free to walk for a few miles. Try not to drink alcohol the night before your Saturday runs. The first four weeks are fairly easy. Week five and beyond become increasingly difficult.
Saturday	**Walk 3 minutes and run 2 minutes. Repeat 6 times.**
Sunday	**Rest.** For beginner runners, this day needs to be kept at a mild rest day. If your body feels good, then go ahead and do some form of cross-training for 30 to 60 minutes.

Tuesday, Wednesday, Thursday: If you can easily hold a conversation with someone, then you are running at the right pace. When you walk, try to maintain a pace no slower than 15 minutes/a mile (4 mph).

Saturdays: Weeks 5-9 will start pushing your limits. Get plenty of sleep the night before. Starting this week, it's important to remember to stretch after your run sessions. If you get tired during a longer duration run, walk for 1/10 mile or 2-3 minutes then speed back up.

Training - Week 7

Monday	**Rest.** Take it easy. Don't run. If you need to exercise, I recommend a walk for no longer than 30 minutes.
Tuesday	**Walk 1 minute and run 4 minutes. Repeat 6 times.**
Wednesday	**Walk 1 minute and run 15 minutes. Repeat 2 times.**
Thursday	**Walk 1 minute and run 4 minutes. Repeat 6 times.**
Friday	**Rest.** Fridays are important rest days. For your muscles to grow stronger, they need rest. Feel free to walk for a few miles. Try not to drink alcohol the night before your Saturday runs. The first four weeks are fairly easy. Week five and beyond become increasingly difficult.
Saturday	**Run 25 minutes.**
Sunday	**Rest.** For beginner runners, this day needs to be kept at a mild rest day. If your body feels good, then go ahead and do some form of cross-training for 30 to 60 minutes.

Tuesday, Wednesday, Thursday: If you can easily hold a conversation with someone, then you are running at the right pace. When you walk, try to maintain a pace no slower than 15 minutes/a mile (4 mph).

Saturdays: Weeks 5-9 will start pushing your limits. Get plenty of sleep the night before. Starting this week, it's important to remember to stretch after your run sessions. If you get tired during a longer duration run, walk for 1/10 mile or 2-3 minutes then speed back up.

Training - Week 8

Monday	**Rest.** Take it easy. Don't run. If you need to exercise, I recommend a walk for no longer than 30 minutes.
Tuesday	**Walk 1 minute and run 4 minutes. Repeat 6 times.**
Wednesday	**Run 20 minutes.**
Thursday	**Walk 1 minute and run 4 minutes. Repeat 6 times.**
Friday	**Rest.** Fridays are important rest days. For your muscles to grow stronger, they need rest. Feel free to walk for a few miles. Try not to drink alcohol the night before your Saturday runs. The first four weeks are fairly easy. Week five and beyond become increasingly difficult.
Saturday	**Run 30 minutes.**
Sunday	**Rest.** For beginner runners, this day needs to be kept at a mild rest day. If your body feels good, then go ahead and do some form of cross-training for 30 to 60 minutes.

Tuesday, Wednesday, Thursday: If you can easily hold a conversation with someone, then you are running at the right pace. When you walk, try to maintain a pace no slower than 15 minutes/a mile (4 mph).

Saturdays: Weeks 5-9 will start pushing your limits. Get plenty of sleep the night before. Starting this week, it's important to remember to stretch after your run sessions. If you get tired during a longer duration run, walk for 1/10 mile or 2-3 minutes then speed back up.

Training - Week 9

Monday	**Rest.** Take it easy. Don't run. If you need to exercise, I recommend a walk for no longer than 30 minutes.
Tuesday	**Walk 3 minutes and Run 2 minutes. Repeat 6 times.**
Wednesday	**Walk 2 minutes and Run 10 minutes. Repeat 3 times.**
Thursday	**Rest.** It's race week. Save up your energy for your 5K race.
Friday	**Rest.** It's race week. Save up your energy for your 5K race. Don't drink alcohol the night before your 5K.
Saturday	**Race Day.**
Sunday	**Rest.**

Tuesday, Wednesday: If you can easily hold a conversation with someone, then you are running at the right pace. When you walk, try to maintain a pace no slower than 15 minutes/a mile (4 mph). Get plenty of sleep. Starting this week, it's important to remember to stretch after your run sessions. If you get tired during a longer duration run, walk for 1/10 mile or 2-3 minutes then speed back up.

Thursday, Friday: Rest both of these days. Do not run. Get plenty of sleep the next two nights before your race on Saturday.

5K Fury

5K Fury - Training Schedule

Week #	Monday	Tuesday	Wednesday	Thursday	Friday	Saturday	Sunday
1	Rest	(W4/R1) × 6	(W4/R1) × 6	(W4/R1) × 6	Rest	(W3/R2)×6	Rest
2	Rest	(W3/R2) × 6	(W3/R2) × 5	(W3/R2) × 6	Rest	(W3/R2)×6	Rest
3	Rest	(W3/R2) × 6	(W2/R4) × 3	(W3/R2) × 6	Rest	(W3/R6) × 3	Rest
4	Rest	(W2/R3) × 6	(W2/R6) × 4	(W2/R3) × 6	Rest	(W3/R8) × 2	Rest
5	Rest	(W2/R3) × 6	(W1/R8) × 3	(W2/R3) × 6	Rest	R12	Rest
6	Rest	(W1/R4) × 6	(W1/R10) × 3	(W1/R4) × 6	Rest	R18	Rest
7	Rest	(W1/R4) × 6	(W1/R15) × 2	(W1/R4) × 6	Rest	R25	Rest
8	Rest	(W1/R4) × 6	R20	(W1/R4) × 6	Rest	R30	Rest
9	Rest	(W3/R2) × 6	(W2/R10) × 3	Rest	Rest	5K	Rest

(i.e. (W2/R6) * 6 = Walk 2 minutes / run 6 minutes repeat 6 times).

A summarized training schedule and log sheet can be downloaded below for FREE:

Go to the web address:
http://geni.us/5KResources

Action Steps

- Stick to your training schedule.
- If you can't run on a given day, change your schedule and don't worry about it.
- Continue walking for at least 10 minutes after a running session.
- Cross training will help you stay active on your non-running days.
- A 30 to 60-minute walk is an excellent source of cross training.

5K Fury

Step 8: Relax the Day Before the Race

Night Before the Race

A lot of people will find it difficult to get enough sleep the night before your first 5K. Some runners will run a few light miles the day before the race. Lay out your running gear so that it will be ready in the morning. This gear includes your clothing, tech gear, waters, gels, hydration packs, water bottles, running shoes, bib, sunglasses, sunblock, headband, and socks. If you picked up your racing runner's packet early, go ahead and pin the racing number on your shirt or shorts. Do not drink alcohol. If you do drink alcohol, limit yourself to a few drinks. Your body will thank you on race day.

5K Fury

Action Steps

- Get all your gear laid out, including clothes, water, phone, phone case Garmins, and Fitbits.
- Attach your bib number to your clothes.
- Know what route you are going to take to the race.
- Keep hydrating.
- Your last dinner before the race shouldn't be a big meal.
- Get at least 7 hours of sleep (might be hard to do this because of anxiety).
- If you are getting edgy or antsy, go for a mile or two walk

Step 9: Get Pumped - It's Race Day

Race Day

The day has finally arrived. Wake up a couple of hours early before the race start time. (Yeah, I know it's early). Eat a small meal as soon as you wake up. This meal should have some carbohydrates, such as a bagel or toast with peanut butter, maybe a few eggs, and water. Avoid high fiber content food. Drink a cup or two of coffee and drink about 12 oz of water before the race. Continue to sip on water leading up to the race. Remember you don't want a sloshing stomach, so don't over drink.

When runners begin to line up for the race, you need to pick the correct starting location in the herd. Do not line up at the front of the starting line unless you are going to run the 5K fast! If you're not planning on running the 5K fast, you need to be back away from the starting line. You could easily get stampeded or hurt someone else if you attempt to be in the front of the line and not race fast. The slowest paced runners such as the walkers need to be in the back of the queue. The average paced runners should be located in the middle of the herd, roughly between the first 20% and 60% of the racers. I have thought, on many occasions, that I was in the correct location somewhere in the middle, and I was wrong. I had to pass many people performing slot type racing just to get out of the muck. The racers at the tail end are planning on walking at a much slower pace. If you need to slow down your pace, then you need to move to the right of the course.

Your blood is pumping, the caffeine is kicking, and the announcer is counting down the last ten seconds before race time. You hear the gun announce the start of the race and you start running way faster than you trained. Take it easy out of the gate. Conserve your energy. Steady and even pacing just like your training will get you to the finish line. You will notice that your pace per mile will be faster than your training pace. The excitement, adrenaline and competitive aspects of the race naturally add to the energy surging through your body. So, take it slow at first and run at the pace you've trained at over the last 9 weeks.

Action Steps

<u>Race day:</u>
- Wake up at least two hours before your race.
- Eat as soon as you get up. Oatmeal, energy bars, and bananas are great sources of food.
- Drink some caffeine 1-2 hours before the race.
- Keep sipping on water up until the race.
- Don't consume too much water. If your stomach is sloshing around, you drank too much - use the restroom.
- Arrive at the race a little early if possible just in case of traffic.

<u>The Race:</u>
- Race like you've trained, and you will finish the race.
- Remember you don't have to run the entire race. Slow down to a brisk walk at the water/aid stations for 1/10 mile or 2 minutes then speed back up.

Step 10: Unwind After the Race

Post-Race

Your body is exhausted, and you might even be a little emotional right now, hanging on to your new, shiny medal, but don't sit down when you cross the finish line. At a bare minimum keep walking for another 5-10 minutes. If your body feels like it, jog at a light pace for another 2-5 minutes. Grab something to drink with electrolytes if possible. You need to eat something within at least one hour after your race, to help replenish your body with nutrients and liquids.

If you're up for it, you can drink a beer or two. Drink plenty of water and keep yourself hydrated over the next couple of days. Sometimes a recovery run the day following your race will help stretch out some of your sore leg muscles. Your recovery run should be at a light pace and not last more than thirty minutes.

I would avoid running for at least 2-3 days to let your legs recover. If your legs are still extremely sore after 3 days, walk a few miles a day until your muscles loosen up before starting to train again.

5K Fury

Action Steps

Post-Race:
- Don't stop moving at the finish line.
- Keep walking for 10 to 20 minutes after the race.
- Grab a sports drink and some food such as a banana, yogurt, or bread.
- Pose for pictures and enjoy your new, shiny medal.
- Stretch your muscles accordingly.
- Don't run for at least 2-3 days.

Conclusion

Congratulations

Pat yourself on the back if you have completed your first 5K. No matter how long it took you to finish your race, remember that you did something awesome today while other people sat on the couch. Congratulations!

Pains and Tweaks

Pains that make you want to stop running. These are different than the minor aches and stiffness you get during your run. Many runs I had to stop and just stretch out to alleviate the stiffness. In fact, my muscles aren't fully warmed up until mile number 2. I have yet to have pains that completely stop my running.

As with any physical activity, no two people are exactly alike. The information provided is an example and a guideline, not an absolute rule that you must follow. Adapt anything to your style to suit your needs as a runner. The two biggest running tips of advice given to me were run naturally and breathe deep. These tips helped me through the long duration runs that can take real effort to complete.

Help an Author Out

Thanks for reading! If you've enjoyed this book, please leave me a short, gleaming review on Amazon. If you're having trouble leaving a review just select one thing you liked about the book. I take the time to read every review so that I can change and update this book based on reviewer feedback.

Go to: http://geni.us/5kFury

If you've just finished your first 5K race and you want someone to tell, send me an email. I would be delighted to hear from you.

Follow me on Facebook and Twitter:

Twitter: @BeginR2FinishR

Facebook: facebook.com/BeginnerToFinisher/

Website: www.halfmarathonforbeginners.com

Email: scottmorton@halfmarathonforbeginners.com

What's Next?

If you want to continue your running career, I urge you to either try to beat your personal best 5K or move on to 10Ks or half marathons. If you have used the training schedules provided in this book, then you should only have to train 6 weeks more to prepare yourself for a 10K. I have full faith that if you crossed the 5K finish line, you could move onto conquering another goal such as a 10K. If you're feeling super ambitious, you can launch into a half marathon training plan. In my #1 Amazon Best Seller Book, Beginner's Guide to Half Marathons, the training plan allows for a 10K race during the 12-week training cycle. You can read this book for FREE with Kindle Unlimited.

Resources

If you're still unsure of where to start or have other questions regarding running for beginners, please read the first book in the series, Beginner to Finisher Book 1:

Why New Runners Fail: 26 Ultimate Tips You Should Know Before You Start Running!

> Go to: **http://geni.us/PaperWhyNewRunnersFail**

You can read for FREE with Kindle Unlimited.
A summarized training schedule and log sheet can be downloaded below for FREE:

FREE 5K training schedule and log sheet

> Go to: **http://geni.us/5KResources**

About the Author

I played sports throughout my youth and even into my adult years. I ran my first 5k at the age of 37 in March of 2008 without any training at all. I finished third place, although my leg muscles felt like I deserved first place. My legs were sore for six days after the race. My next 5k attempt was in 2015 at the age of 42 in my local hometown. I had no intention of placing at all. I ended up running worse than my first 5k by almost two minutes. I placed second with no training at all. I thought I would have learned a lesson by now - nope.

In May 2016, I was flying to Las Vegas for our yearly guys' trip. I was reading a *Sky Mall* magazine, and I came across an article called "Top 100 things to do in Las Vegas." Number eight on the list was run a race through the streets of Las Vegas. During the race, the city blocks off sections of the strip. I was hooked. They offered a 5k, 10k, half marathon and marathon. I liked walking a lot; in fact, one of my favorite things to do in Las Vegas was to see how many steps I could get in a day (my record to date is 42,000). The Rock-and-Roll Half Marathon/Marathon would be taking place in November 2016. I scoured the Internet for any information related to training for a half marathon.

My wife asked me, "Why in the world do you want to run a half marathon?" I told her because I was physically able to. She said, "You just want to put one of those 13.1 stickers on the back of your car." But truthfully the real reason was much deeper than that. Whenever I catch a fresh dump of powder on my snowboard, there is no other experience like it. I feel like a kid again, and I feel alive. The real reason I wanted to run was that I wanted to feel the accomplishment, feel the pain and feel the glory of crossing the finish line all the while feeling alive. Running allows me to unleash that competitive kid inside me who yearns to feel alive.

For a special sneak peek of,

Why New Runners Fail: 26 Ultimate Tips You Should Know Before You Start Running,
(Book #1 in the Series Beginner to Finisher),
turn to the next page.

For the Ebook version go to:

http://geni.us/EbookWhyNewRunnersFail

For the paperback version go to:

http://geni.us/PaperWhyNewRunnersFail

For the audiobook version go to:

http://geni.us/AudioWhyNewRunnersFail

Not Running Enough

Running too little will not allow your body to get used to a training schedule. For example, let's say that you only run two days a week—let's pick Monday and Thursday—to run. Each session consists of 1 mile running followed by 1 mile of walking.

Negatives:
- Your body isn't getting used to running.
- You might be more susceptible to injury because your body isn't able to rebuild and reuse the muscles quickly enough. It's almost like your body is forgetting how to run between workouts.
- You won't be able to progress much further than your training mileage.
- Inadequate running makes the mental struggle harder on the mind. Your mind and body think they are being reset after each run session and are not learning the habit of running.

Positives:
- You are exercising.

I don't think that you should ever drop below an absolute minimum of three days running/walking. I prefer at least four days of running. If you decide to run a maximum of three days, I highly suggest that you skip every other day (see below).

Three days of training

Monday	Tuesday	Wednesday	Thursday	Friday	Saturday	Sunday
Run	Rest	Run	Rest	Run	Rest	Walk

Four days of training (Preferred)

Monday	Tuesday	Wednesday	Thursday	Friday	Saturday	Sunday
Run	Run	Rest	Run	Rest	Run	Walk

Action Steps
- Running too little makes it tougher on your body than having a normal running schedule.
- Don't run less than 3 times a week if you want to progress in the sport of running.

WHY NEW RUNNERS FAIL

26 ULTIMATE TIPS YOU SHOULD KNOW BEFORE YOU START RUNNING

SCOTT O. MORTON

For a special sneak peek of,

Beginner's Guide to Half Marathons: A Simple Step-By-Step Solution to Get You to the Finish Line in 12 Weeks! (Book #4 in the Series Beginner to Finisher), turn to the next page.

Beginner's Guide to Half Marathons has become an Amazon #1 Bestseller.

For the Ebook version go to:

http://geni.us/EbookHalfMarathons

For the paperback version go to:

http://geni.us/PaperHalfMarathons

For the audiobook version go to:

http://geni.us/AudioHalfMarathons

The runner's mindset. Getting past the fear of running 13.1 miles is one of the biggest hurdles of completing a half marathon. I'm going to let you in on a big secret that helped me get past my fear of having to run 13.1 miles. The secret is that most runners don't run the entire 13.1 miles. Wow, what a secret. It's true. The super athletes and other runners trying to beat their personal best records might very well run the entire race. However, I have completed three half marathons and one full marathon, and the majority of runners will walk through the water/aid stations along the course. Once I realized that you don't have to run the entire distance, the fear of running a half marathon vanished, instantly. My mind had found a chink in the armor. Once I exploited the weakness of the 13.1 half marathon beast, my mindset changed forever on long-distance running. This same technique allowed me to complete a marathon as well. Someone reading this right now is probably saying, "He's probably been running for a long time." I was able to complete three half marathons and one full marathon over the course of a year. I began in May 2016 and completed my third half marathon on April 22, 2017, at the age of 43 with no prior long distance running experience whatsoever. I'm by no means a super athlete, just an average person with high beliefs that I could finish a half marathon. I hope that this encourages you to finish your first half marathon no matter what age you begin at. If I can do it, so can you.

Finishing a 5K or a 10K can be easily accomplished with little or no training at all. If your goal is to run or walk/run a half marathon, then you must tell yourself that you are a runner. You are no longer running for the sake of exercise. You are running to train your body to complete your first half marathon. You are now training for a half marathon.

Many things that I go over in this book are solely my opinion. Every training schedule discussed within this book has been used by me to complete three half marathons and a full marathon. There are several different schools of thought when it comes to how much running per week it takes to train for a half marathon. There are different nutrition guides, shoe strategies, running miles per week, etc. There is, however, one common thing agreed upon by almost all runners - you have to believe in yourself and believe that you are a runner. Without this firmly ingrained in your head, you won't make it past mile nine, and you won't make it to the finish line. I'm not telling you this to discourage you. I'm telling you this to prepare you for the mental battle of running. One week at a time, one day at a time, one mile at a time, and one step at a time will get you to the half marathon finish line.

BEGINNER'S GUIDE TO HALF MARATHONS

A SIMPLE STEP-BY-STEP SOLUTION TO GET YOU TO THE FINISH LINE IN 12 WEEKS!

SCOTT O. MORTON

Other Books by Scott Oscar Morton

If you would like to know when I publish my new Ebook releases, please sign up by clicking here. All books can be read for FREE with Kindle Unlimited.

Beginner to Finisher Series:

Available Now:
Book 1: *Why New Runners Fail: 26 Ultimate Tips You Should Know Before You Start Running!*
Book 2: *5K Fury: 10 Proven Steps to Get You to the Finish Line in 9 weeks or less!*
Book 4: *Beginner's Guide to Half Marathons: A Simple Step-By-Step Solution to Get You to the Finish Line in 12 Weeks!*

Coming Soon:
Book 3: *10K Titan: A Proven system to start properly training for your long runs!*
Book 5: *Marathon Motivator: A Simple Step-By-Step Solution to get you to the Finish line in 20 Weeks!*

Printed in Great Britain
by Amazon